MW00618311

BROKEN FREQUENCIES

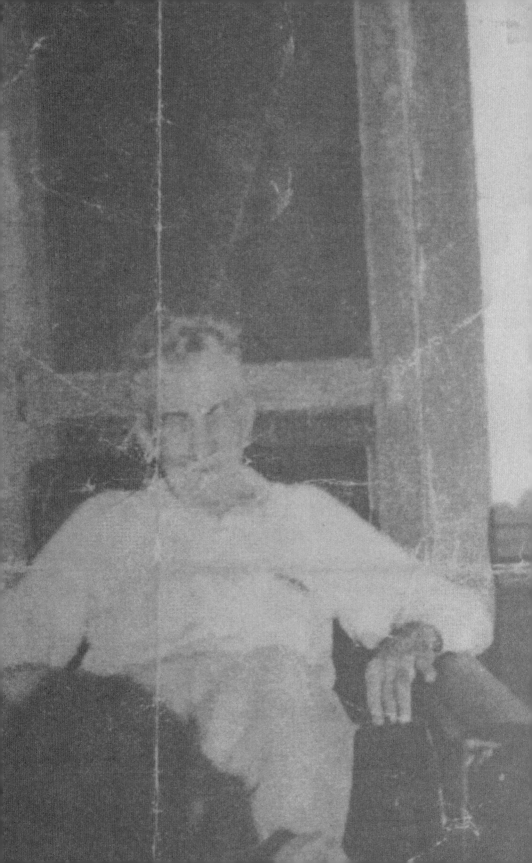

BROKEN FREQUENCIES

a book of poems

J A M E S   A L A N   R I L E Y

SHADELANDHOUSE MODERN PRESS
LEXINGTON, KENTUCKY

BROKEN FREQUENCIES
a book of poems

For information about permission to reproduce selections from
this book, please direct written inquiries to
Permissions, Shadelandhouse Modern Press, LLC,
P.O. Box 910913, Lexington, KY 40591

Published 2019 in the United States by:
    Shadelandhouse Modern Press, LLC
    Lexington, Kentucky
    smpbooks.com

Shadelandhouse, Shadelandhouse Modern Press, and the colo-
phon are trademarks of Shadelandhouse Modern Press, LLC.

First edition

Library of Congress Control Number: 2018956786
ISBN 978-1-945049-13-2

Printed and manufactured in the United States of America
Book design and page layout: Benjamin Jenkins
Cover design: Benjamin Jenkins
Cover art: *Stripes* by Artem Chebokha
Used by permission
Title Page photograph © James Alan Riley
Used by permission

Production Editor: Stephanie Pistello

for Tammy

Contents

I

In a World Without Birds

They know a bird when they see one.
They recognize feathers and wings,
but that's about as far as they can go

beyond the different colors, the red one
and the blue one or the black,
the generic woodpecker or chicken.

In a world without birds, all ducks
are the same duck quacking in circles
on some stagnant, unkept pond.

No Red-winged Blackbirds rise from the cattails
to scatter their thoughts in alarm.
No Mockingbirds sing from their telephone poles.

There is no Robin or House Wren,
no White-streaked Sparrow,
Tufted Titmouse or Common Crow.

God forbid a Towhee land in the azaleas
behind their house as the temperature drops,
the first call of winter a whistle.

The limbs of their Sycamore trees
blister in silence on summer mornings,
the hush of evening already fallen.

Spring doesn't drift above their dandelions.
Hope doesn't nest in their hedgerows.
Death doesn't pick through their garbage. ☆

Self Portrait with Old Man

I

Coming from that world to this
requires a certain skill in brutality.
There is no mercy in a world
where shadows cross the night sky
in slow, gliding motions.

He should be wearing something
more appropriate for the occasion
than a pair of ragged jeans,
a worn-out Guinness hoodie
with a hole in the sleeve.
His wife warns him all the time
about going out in public
without combing his hair.
"You never know who you'll meet,"
she says, "or who'll be taking pictures."

He eyes the smooth surface of the water,
the reflection of tall trees at his feet.
There is a ripple among the water lilies.

II

There is a ripple among the water lilies.
You can tell from the expression
on his face that he clings to that hope,
feels the weight of it in his hands
as if there were some other way
to measure the depth of sorrow.

There is the color of tree.
There is the color of sky.
Looks can be as deceiving as any doubt
caught between what came before
and a color so casual and sad.
Hope is the water at his feet.

III

Hope is the water at his feet.
How else might this end
with so much green rising
from the shadows and light?
He does not understand such motion
through the trees, the wild grass
that grows along the bank,
the good fortune of a cautious approach.

And when he gets down on his knees,
there is only the long shadow
of big birds crossing the sky,
their blue reflections smooth
above that still surface.

IV

Above that still surface,
he gazes into the distance
as if there were something beyond
all this green and wide water,
beyond even the wet ground
at his feet. The water cools.
The light fades. Even now,
he does not understand

there are those who think all this
will end as the moment moves beyond
the reach of his outstretched hand.
The hardest part is always the letting go.
The absence of hope is shallow water.

V
The absence of hope is shallow water,
the long shadow of a heron poised,
motionless, patient and waiting.
Wind crosses the surface in small waves.
Light reflects the blue and broken sky.
Loss rises from the water and takes flight.

The world is full of long shadows,
a parchment of colors gone gray.
Do not mistake the voice you hear
calling from across that wide water.
Do not mistake suffering for relief. ☆

Ghost Story

When I was a young man
and my oldest son was three,
we lived in a house haunted
by an old woman. She wasn't rude
or abusive, but it was obvious
she didn't want us living
in her house. She would do things,
send vines through the bedroom
window at night and twist them slowly
through the rails of the baby's crib
as if they were wrapping around a neck.
One night, she turned the pilot light off
on the gas stove in the living room.
Each of her warnings got my attention,
but she had other ways of making her point.

I fought an onslaught of creatures
when we lived in that house. Hornets
came swarming down from the attic.
A mischief of rats moved into the kitchen.
Brown recluse spiders. When the traps
stopped working, I killed the rats
by hand with a broom handle, standing
motionless in the dark kitchen
and spearing their heads as they passed.

I carried their quivering bodies by the tail,
their smashed heads dripping blood.
Reality can be gruesome, and I hated
those rats, but the spiders were worse,
creeping along the baseboards of our bedroom

walls at night, watching us as we slept.
I would see them if I turned on the light,
but they were quick and silent, slipping
into the nearest crevice as if their existence
were a matter only of perception.

I tell this story as true from the comfort
of two lifetimes away. My son is grown
and has two children of his own,
but I remember living in that house.
I remember standing on the front porch
and watching it rain, the future reflected
in pools of water as an old man rose
from one of the many possible untold versions. ☆

Theories of Elegance

I

I remember the sky in Kentucky at night
cut from the horizon and hung before
the stars like comfort and desire,
our singular need for assurance.

We are told there are, in most cases,
not one star but two, lovers in constant motion
one around the other, but light too often refracts.
Distance, like memory, can be deceiving.

And so it seems that even the stars are paired,
locked in mutual rotations and whirling
through the universe in strange harmonies
we could never imagine.

II

Always before, when a star fell,
I thought, meteorite if it strikes
the ground among these brown hills,
otherwise, we say meteor. Either way,
the dark sky would be suddenly bright,
a camera flash behind the eyes,
and when the darkness returned, the image
reappeared of my hand reaching out
before me. It is an image of myself,
the shadow of a tree beside the house,
our lives together, the unexpected truth
in a field of lies.

III

I have learned the best theories
are descriptive in nature. They offer
no truth or explanation, only abstract notions
of elegance which apply to both distance
and proximity, a fraction derived
from the same common denominator, coming
and going as if light and heat
were a product, one from the other,
caught in a constant motion
but never striking the ground.

IV

When we met that first night, it rained so hard
you couldn't call it weather, precipitation
as the children are taught to say in school, the word
a mouthful of marbles. The rain became for us

environment. We felt our way through darkness
unaware that even the sky might fall
if we turned away long enough not to notice.
Lightning always gathers momentum.

The next morning, I found its jagged scar
on an oak so thick I could have put my arms
around the fractured trunk and found nothing.
Harmony is nature's only true desire.

Lightning never strikes the ground.
It rises like an outstretched hand,
a diffraction of separate charges
come together in a moment of sight.

V

How do we explain such strange phenomenon,
this summer lightning when there are no clouds?
A positive theory of negative circumstance?
Good and evil in a binary flux of ions?
The warmth rises and glows on a horizon
spreading slow against a chamomile sky.
I touch your warm skin and settle
beneath the sheet. What arguments exist
for these lights that whisper us together,
calling us away from this Kentucky farm house
on this summer night? The only need I feel
for explanation has been explained
by the touch of your hand.
Theory cannot save us from ourselves.
We must sacrifice our bodies
to see by our own light. ☆

Love in the Many Worlds

I
A leaf drifts from the hillside behind the house,
unloosed as air in the uncertain world.
What is and is not possible listens
to that quiet motion, event horizons of Mimosa
and White Pine, the beginning and the end.

The body lifts and falls in slow rotation,
weightless in a verse where there is no
definitive line, the evening calmed by shadows
warm as the touch of your hand.

These are the moments that define us—
I sometimes forget.

II
I remember when we were young,
lying on a blanket in the yard
and staring at the night sky.

Overhead, a meteor shower flashed
in random bright moments before our eyes,
a trail of light crossing the dark sky,
then burning out.

Not stars, exactly, but the stuff of stars
pulled from the unknown universe to the known
by some inevitable force of mutual attraction,
the gravity of being caught so completely
in one another's arms.

There are no right answers to some questions.
Have we come together by chance or are these waves
we ride as we burn through the atmosphere?

III

I hurt your feelings once when I said
I didn't believe in soul mates.
"There's no such thing," I said, realizing,
even as I spoke, that I was wrong.

The future and the past are connected
in mysterious ways. It is important
to know which question to ask of a moment
both lost and found, the spark
of singular attraction a paradox.

This cloud that clings to the last
rays of light from the sun, this leaf
that drifts through time and space,
they are both numbered yet numberless.

If one is the starting point,
how can two be anything less than infinite?
Who, between us, does not hold
the beginning of all things in one hand
and the end of all things in the other,
where we are and where we are going
measured in small disappointments
balanced on the edge of forgiveness.

IV

I almost drowned when I was a child.
I stepped without knowing into the deep end
and found myself at the bottom of the pool.
I remember the water rising around me
in shafts of light. I remember the mystery
of being unable to breathe and the sudden
realization that all things must end.

Heavy metals are the burden of youth.

And then a hand took hold of my hand
and pulled me back to this world,
the world where we would sit, years later,
and watch leaves fall in the yard.

There was no accident that day.
I was pulled from that world to this
as if all the many worlds possible
offered but the one possibility,
the world of fire and the world of water
a dream only of what might have been
compared to this night filled with stars.

V

Is there a world where we are not together?
Is there a world where we are together again?
Falling and watching someone fall from a distance
are two completely different things.
The leaves in the trees, the stars in the sky,
their very atoms lie in the palms of our hands,
a remnant from some other place in time,
the long ago and far away of our lives before
we found ourselves falling into eternity. ☆

In the Garden of Unknown Things

The garden is overgrown with weeds,
the tomatoes hanging like empty sacks.
My mother stares out the window.
She is trying to remember the word *deer*.
She tells me again how when she was little,
she thought the Japanese army was on the outskirts
of Ponca City. "I didn't want to go to school,"
she says. "I wanted to stay home but Daddy
wouldn't let me. He said the Japanese
didn't want nothing to do with Oklahoma.
He said we didn't have nothing to bomb but dirt."

She smiles like a child, and I think
this too must be received, having come
to the edge of night, the moon unable
to leap. My mother is trying to remember
the word *orange,* her world gone mysterious
and strange. She is staring out the window
at a deer in the garden. I know that look
like I know the touch of her hand.
It is the look she gave me when I left
the hospital the night my father died.
He had been her husband for fifty years.
"How was I to know he would skip out on me,"
she says as if dying were the same as going
to the store for a loaf of bread.

"Would you like something to eat?"
I ask. "Are you hungry?"
"When I was a little girl," she says,
"the only thing we got for Christmas

was a piece of fruit." I butter toast
and pour another cup of coffee.
Her fork scrapes against her plate.
My mother is trying to remember the word *egg*.
The garden is full of weeds.
I fill the sink with soap and water.
"Who is that man washing dishes?" she asks.
"It's just me, Mom," I say, "your son."
"Oh," she says smiling, "I thought that's who you were." ☆

Home Movies

I

I am falling in circles, chasing
a puppy we got from a litter
an old woman kept in a drawer
filled with rags and worn socks.
My baby sister has just been born.
I stop, turn to the camera
and shield my eyes from the sun.
I am smiling in yellows
and soft browns, the faded
sepia of all those years.

II

A jagged sequence of faces
smiling in soft focus, a sidebar
of sprocket holes and I am sitting
at a kitchen table in the house
on Center Street, an angel food cake
before me with white icing
lit by five burning candles.
I look like my oldest son's child
in the soft light from the candles.
My mother leans into the frame.
She smiles and waves and pushes
a strand of black hair behind her ear.

III

There comes a time when the images
pass so quickly they carry no sense
of time or place, a young boy swinging
a toy golf club, a dog running in circles.

My brother chases a butterfly with a net.
There is a sprinkler in the yard
and we are taking turns running
through a spray of cold water.
My mother is wearing a summer dress
and white bobby socks. She is laughing
with her head back and her eyes closed.

IV

"I can't take this anymore," my brother says. "I just want to
    lie down and go to sleep and not wake up. You know what I
    mean?"

 "Have you been drinking?" I ask.

"A little," he says, "a half-pint of tequila."

"Well, don't drink too much," I say. "We'll figure it out
    tomorrow."

"What's to figure out? They want twenty thousand dollars or she
    has to go. I don't have twenty thousand dollars."

"What they want and what they get are two different things," I
    say. "They have to care for her."

"I can't do this anymore," my brother says. "I'm done. Remember
    when you had to bury our dog? I couldn't handle a dead dog.
    How the hell am I supposed to handle this?"

V

I am driving a truck with no muffler,
a brown paper sack in the seat beside me
as I cross the river bridge.
It is a clear night with no moon,
the stars displaced above an open field
of soybeans and cotton. I have just come
from the vet who assured me he would be happy
to dispose of the body for a small fee.

"No, thanks," I say. "That won't be necessary."

I had no plan when I started across the bridge,
saw the river stretching into the distance
on both sides, the dark current below.

I pulled to the shoulder of the road,
got out and leaned against the rail.
The paper sack in my hand hardly
weighed more than the sack itself,
life's final truths all but weightless.
And then I held the sack out over the rail
and let it drop. It fell in a slow
turning circle through a long silence,
falling and falling until it hit the water. ☆

The Heart's Sad Music

I

Their voices rise from our past
in a sudden moment of waking, harmony
before harmonies were thought to exist.
It happens all the time.

You reach for the phone. Sometimes
you have the phone in your hand
and you're dialing the number before
you realize what you've done.

You stop dialing. You put the phone down.
We are surrounded by the ghosts of those we love.

II

I was on my way to the funeral home
when I stopped to visit with Mom.
I found her sitting in her wheelchair,
her hands folded in her lap.

Sometimes she recognizes me
and sometimes she doesn't.
I never know which it will be.

"You just missed Jesse," she says.
"She came by to visit for a while."

"That was nice of her," I say.
I don't mention that her sister Jesse
has been dead twenty years. I smile
and ask how Jesse is doing these days.

"She's one hot mess," Mom says. "You know Jesse."

"Yes," I say. "She always was."

"What about your daddy?" Mom says.
"Have you seen your daddy?"

I don't remind her again that Daddy
passed away seven years ago.
"It's been a while," I say,
bracing myself for what I know is coming.

Mom looks at me as if she knows something
she shouldn't know, as if the air itself
has been whispering in her ear.

"What about your sister Renee?" she says.
"She was supposed to come see me but she hasn't."
Her fingers pick at the blanket in her lap.

"I haven't seen Renee," I say, trying
to be honest. "I'm not sure where she is."

III
From the balcony of the Days Inn
I can see the green exit sign on the four-lane.
There is a Taco Bell and a McDonald's below,
the sound of trucks passing in the distance.

My brother is sitting on an unmade bed
in the room behind me, the door open.

He is drinking a beer at eight in the morning.
My older sister is in the parking lot.
She is getting out of her new minivan,
unloading a single overnight bag.
When she sees me, she waves.

My little sister is down the road
about a mile. There are old photographs
playing in an endless loop on the wall
above her body. There are pictures
of us all when we were young, a picture
of Daddy holding a golf club,
of Mom in a yellow straw hat.

There are mostly pictures of Renee.
In one, she is wearing a silk gown,
her high school graduation picture.
In another she is sitting on a horse
whose name I can't recall.

"Well?" my older sister says as she joins me
on the balcony of the Days Inn.
The passing trucks echo in the distance.
"Did you tell Mom about Renee?"

"No," I say, "I tried to tell her
but I couldn't. It wasn't a good time."
My sister frowns the frown she uses
not for displeasure but disdain.
"Whatever," she says. "When do you think
will be a good time?"

"I don't know," I say. "I was thinking
maybe we should let Renee tell her."

"That's not funny," my sister says.

IV
Years before we put Mom in the nursing home,
before they told us she was worse than we thought
and moved her to the dementia ward,
my brother and I took her
to the Crater of Diamonds State Park
in Murfreesboro, Arkansas.
THE BEST KEPT SECRET IN THE SOUTH,
the sign said as we drove into town.

Mom was as excited as I've ever seen her,
a seventy-four-year-old woman digging for diamonds
with a garden trowel in a plowed field.
Sifting the loose dirt through her fingers,
her only protection was the wide brim of her hat.

"We shouldn't be looking for diamonds," I say.
"We should be looking for shade."

"It's not hot," Mom says.
When I couldn't convince her to stop,
I took a picture of her smiling
beneath the brim of her straw hat.

V

Where else might our dreams take us
but to the people we have always loved?
They rise from our memories like a song
caught between the moment we reach
for the phone and the moment we realize
no one is going to answer.

There is no easy way to say this.
We smile and wave to the camera.
We face forward as we drift
into a past whose only harmony rises
from the things we should have said
in the silence between photographs. ☆

Playing My Brother's Guitar

There are some melodies
we have no choice but suffer,
the rhythm of absence rising
from the nylon strings
of my brother's guitar,
the weight of it in my arms.

I never know where to begin.
The only songs I know are old songs,
lyrics aged by forgetfulness and loss:
You shouldn't drink so much.
You should take better care of yourself.
A string rattles on the wrong fret.
I stop, go back to the beginning,
begin again.

I am trying to play a song
I cannot play, trying to explain
something that cannot be explained.
The rhythm stops and starts.
I don't know what else to do.
The only songs we ever knew
were the mistakes we made,
songs the color of fallen leaves,
the sepia and amber, the burnt
and the umber and the orange.
I am playing a song in the key
of worst possible scenarios,
a song on a brown guitar. ☆

An Amateur's Guide to the Migratory Flight of Birds

If there is a pattern, I have not found it,
though I can hear them high in the winter sky
like the notes of some minor scale tilting
always toward the horizon.

> *Once the Eastern Towhee migration begins,*
> *they can fly continuously for days,*
> *the length of their journey unmeasured*
> *though considered one of the most ambitious.*

Every journey looks easy from the point
of arrival, having crossed the latitude
of myth with the longitude of unknown things.
The mystery lies in the silence between notes.

> *Thousands of Red-winged Blackbirds*
> *have been falling dead from the sky*
> *over a small town in Eastern Kentucky.*
> *Many consider this a sign of something ominous.*

The nursing home called this evening to say
they had moved my mother to the dementia wing.
Wouldn't it be something to always know
where you were in relation to where you should be?

> *Crows recognize individual facial features.*
> *If you feed them, they will wait and watch*
> *for you, not just for anyone, but you.*
> *The Common Crow is considered non-migratory.*

When I stepped outside this morning, crows
scattered through the trees like scraps of paper.
Their silhouettes against the melting snow
sat high up in my mind, calling to me and calling,
but when I turned to look, I saw only bare branches.

> *Nature plays a role in successful migration.*
> *Birds with reduced sensibilities, poor eyesight,*
> *loss of mobility, can become disoriented and find*
> *themselves far from their planned destinations.*

Last night, there were seagulls scattered
across the parking lot of the Wal-Mart
in Pikeville, Kentucky, their white bodies
resting among the frozen piles of snow.
They might have been floating on water
in the melted patches of wet concrete,
and I thought, What chance do the rest of us
have against the pull of such gravity?
Toward what harmony does the past linger
when we have no choice but settle for discontent? ☆

II

Broken Frequencies

Do you remember that night?
The ghost in the room moved like a shadow between us.

And was that shadow reaching for us from the dark window?
Delivering a message on some other frequency,
which, even at its simplest, was never clear,
garbled with static and interference as it skimmed
the surface of what was meant for music.

And were we not going there together?
We might have missed each other entirely
were it not for your hand in mine,
the first stone in place, assuring the very stars align
not from beyond but from within the human heart.

Is there not at least one universe in each of our memories?
The sense of all endings are for those who do not understand
the nature of the story being told, who suspect ever after
only to realize there is no such thing in the sudden motion
of a hand rising, the stars falling in streaks across the night sky,
a testament to what is possible when someone raises one hand
to stay the inevitable.

*That we might live our lives never knowing with certainty the answer
to that first question?*
Do we not see ourselves in those who came before us
and those who follow? What were those brief moments
but the years we watched burn slowly from beyond the motion
of our lives? Are we not still in motion, the girl I cannot reach
yet cannot forget? I see you from the hillside where I wait,
from the yard where we once sat on a blanket and measured
our own sense of eternity passing. ☆

Winter Song

An old man sits and plays his guitar.
He is playing a tune in the key of summer
for a boy who reminds him of childhood.

Cold scratches at the window
but the song is warm.
It is a song of summer.

The old man and the boy dance in their socks.
They have been building a snowman
with rocks for eyes and a crooked smile.

The snowman whistles the only tune he knows
as wind sweeps the yard in white gusts.
The thought of spring drifts against the fence.

Crows leave their jagged tracks in the snow
like random notes. The bare trees sing in silence:
What we sometimes find beautiful can also be dire.

But not for the old man and the boy.
They dance as if dancing were a song,
ignoring, for now, the tuneless crows,
the snowman's sinister grin. ☆

Lazarus Rising: The Tao of Goldfish

for Kaden

I

Infinity swims in a twenty-gallon tank
at Wal-Mart. The boy studies each fish.
You call that pretty good odds.

II

His given name is Squiggles
but mostly he goes by his biblical name.
Is it not somehow more appropriate?

III

The secret to longevity is the perfect balance
of dead flies ground to a fine powder.
Longevity is the myth of just a pinch.

IV

If Squiggles is a pseudonym
for eternal life,
Lazarus is the Now.

V

You know with grave certainty
that this too is reality
in the eyes of a child.

VI

If life swims, death floats,
which proves, if nothing else,
the short life-span of any given fish.

VII

"I wish fish didn't have to die."
"They don't," you say as if amazed.
You are nothing if not quick with the net.

VIII

"He's not dead. He's only sleeping.
See how peacefully he drifts, motionless
on just the surface of the water."

IX

If a dead fish is reality,
a fish that swims is truth.

X

Is it coincidence that all fish look alike?
Only if you plan ahead.

XI

Question: What are you doing after work?
Answer: Going to Wal-Mart.

XII

The burial of the dead is a secret ritual.
Rising from the dead is also a secret ritual.

XIII

Squiggles sinks like a stone.
Weep not beside still waters.
Lazarus has risen. ☆

The Weight of Gravity
and Great Distance

I

The boy is picking dandelions in the yard,
wish flowers, he calls them, but if you tell
anyone your wish, it won't come true.
"That seems fair," I say and make a wish.
The seeds scatter across the yard,
my wish tucked away for safe keeping
as the possibilities drift beyond reach,
floating on the hope that gravity
will eventually pull even the lightest
of them to the ground, as if wishes
were weightless and capable of flight.

II

I had a recurring dream as a child.
In the dream, my family was sitting
in a dark room when a light appeared
beneath the couch, a light only I could see.
It moved along the edge of the rug
until, eventually, it touched
each member of my family, one by one,
first my grandfather and then my grandmother,
my father and then my mother.
It was a nightmare, and when I cried out,
my mother would come to my bed
and promise that dreams were not real.

"You don't have to worry about such,"
she said. "That's a long time away."

I was six the year I made my mother
get out bed every night, the boy's age now.
I watch him playing in the yard, picking
dandelions as if they were daisies,
but when he calls me to his bed at night,
his dreams filled with monsters,
I cannot help but think of the nightmare
I had as a child and how it came true
despite my mother's promise
there was no such thing as monsters.

I offer this same assurance to the boy,
though I can feel the warm weight of my mother
sitting beside me in the dark bedroom.

III
Could there be a more genuine act of grace
than the having of what we always wanted
but could never have? I reach across the bed
and touch your shoulder. *Are you asleep?*
Some moments live in our memories
like the soft edge of an afternoon,
a child's voice calling our name.

I do not imagine the concern in your voice
when you sit up and ask about the boy.
There is no discussion when all our fears
have been decided for us, whispering
these are days made not to be forgotten.
I reach across the bed. I touch your shoulder.
For whatever reason undeserved, this is where

we are, despite the regret we cannot escape,
the dream of our lives together both as distant
and as close as your hand taking hold of my hand.

IV
What comfort there is in this world
is the comfort of hope.

V
Evening settles across the yard.
The wish flowers are blooming,
their white parachutes whispering
the many possible miracles of a single breath.
The child we are raising who isn't ours.
The child we wanted but could never have.

Beneath the weight of gravity
and great distance, I keep my wishes
to myself. I reach across the bed,
touch your warm shoulder.
There are times when just a touch
is enough to ease the slow descent. ☆

The Snowman

An old man looks out his window.
We see the old man but we cannot see
out the window where a tree grows.

The wind is blowing
because the leaves
in the tree are moving.
Snow begins to fall.

The old man is watching the snow fall
when he realizes there are no leaves
in the tree nor wind to move them.
There is only the shadow of a bare
branch on the white ground.

The man standing at the window
thought there were leaves.
He thought the wind was blowing
because the leaves in the tree
were moving, but then there were
no leaves, the snow falling in silence.

We watch the old man at the window
but we cannot see what the old man sees.
He thought there were leaves and,
for a moment, there were leaves,
but then a child came and built a snowman
beneath the shadow of a bare branch. ☆

Skunkie's Dead

for J.S.

I can still hear her motor
running off in the distance
from my grandma's porch
in Oceola, Arkansas.
It is the summer of 1962,
before the world we all knew died,
and then there she is,
turning the corner and coming
across the dirt-packed playground
of the Warren G. Harding Elementary School
on her scooter, the pop and rattle
of her engine whining
as she gives it the gas
and lets it unwind.

I was a sophomore
and she was a senior,
her brown legs mythic
in a pair of cutoff jeans,
that shock of white hair
pushed back from her face
as she slid in the gravel
of my grandma's driveway
and came to a stop
in the yard.

It was the hair that did it,
gave her the name she could never shake,
even now, as I read the e-mail,
forty-five years and three states away
from my grandma's porch

in Oceola, Arkansas:
Skunkie's dead. She died
last night in her sleep.

I imagine her lying in Houston, Texas
with her grieving husband and children gathered,
and I think, *Skunkie's dead.*
But for me that's not quite true,
having loved the sound of that motor scooter
coming across the playground of Harding Elementary
like a wave of water, like the whole rest
of my wasted sophomore days, her hand
reaching out for me as if to say,
"Hop on and I'll give you a ride." ☆

Thoreau's Cell Phone

I'm not saying he wouldn't
have taken it with him,
but it's nice to think
he might have gone without,
passed on the opportunity to shoot
a few pics of the pond in winter
and written about it instead,
the occasional loon drifting
over nine perfect rows of beans.

Who knows? He may not have been able
to live without it, the quiet evenings
more agreeable reading text messages,
Facebooking his BFF for personal assistance
should worse come to worse:
Wassup?
Reading. U?
Jail.
WTFGDA.

I imagine the long nights
tough with nothing to do
but plank the woodpile
or meme some angled shot
of his own bare buttocks
#moonoverwalden.

He might even have done without
on occasion, stuck with no bars
or his battery charging, and walked
to town for a little FaceTime

about the changing nature
of the English language
#WTF
#☺

These Ghosts

I have only empirical knowledge
to work with but from what I've seen,
the dead are a fairly dispirited bunch,
indifferent for the most part,
apathetic to a fault, and more
than just a little obsessive-compulsive,
turning all the light switches off and on,
rattling door knobs as they come and go.

The presence of someone's dead grandmother
is a deal breaker in most books
on the art of real estate,
the list of have and have nots
disallowing old men with chains
rising from the ground, slothful
and indolent, dare I say it—lazy?

Opening doors and rocking in empty chairs,
they rarely concern themselves
with the business of daily living.
Try rattling a pipe wrench
for a change, you think, *try making*
yourself useful. Has no one but me
noticed the grass hasn't been mown,
the weeds grown wild beneath the roses?
Would a little help with the laundry
be too much to ask? Sort the colors
from the whites while you're milling about
at all hours in the dark of night.
Were those dishes not in the sink
when I went to bed last night?

One would hope the dead
would be a little more motivated,
but that doesn't seem to be the case,
moping their mopes, languishing
in some false nostalgia for the past.

Small wonder they lack motivation,
they keep such odd hours, skulking
about the house with nothing better to do
than linger at the top of the stairs.
In what world is passing through walls
for no reason not loitering?
And why is the answer to the question
What's that banging around in the kitchen?
never, *Oh, that's just Grandma Rainbolt*
mopping the kitchen floor again. ☆

Leonardo at the Kitchen Table

When once you have tasted flight,
you will forever walk the earth
with your eyes turned skyward.

—Leonardo da Vinci

Some things are so simple you have to smile,
thinking maybe you should have a glass of wine,
and then you look up and realize Leonardo
is sitting at the kitchen table, cyphering
his cyphers like a total goof. "With ears
like those," you say, "I'm surprised
you're not doing the math in your head."
He knows what you mean. You mean physiognomy
has been a joke for six hundred years, and then
you realize you're the only one laughing.

There is water running under the house.
A pipe has frozen and burst.
Leonardo has stopped working to listen
with his ginormous ears, his pencil poised
above some contraption that may or may not fly
once pushed, or flung, from the nearest rampart.
"There are those of us who fly," he says,
"and there are those of us who plumb."
Nothing crashes faster than an abstract theory
in a time of war, or shatters quite like glass.

So now you're thinking, *What-ev, bromeister,*
but that's not what you say.
You say, "The 15th Century called.
They want their doodles back."

He knows what you mean. You mean
we have no need for flying mechanicals here.
Lift formulas and weight ratios need not apply.
He shakes his head as if to infer your problem
is one of which theory has washed its hands,
there being but one solution in a land without ramparts:
If the meat goes bad, you must begin again.

He may be known for his intelligence,
but his lack of empathy is staggering.
You want to say *If that's supposed to make
me feel better, it's not working.* Meanwhile,
your water bill is being multiplied
by the speed of light.
Leonardo gives you a confused look.
"Earth to Leonardo," you say, "Come in, Leonardo."
But what you're thinking is *Help me out
on this one, brainiac.* You're not asking
for a chart of the human endocrine system.
You don't need impossible bridge architecture.

There are times when what you need
is something a little less substantial
than human anatomy or medieval mechanics,
something to keep your wet fingers from freezing
while you're under the house with a vice-grip.
Get with the program, dude, you want to say
at the risk of sounding culturally deprived.
But some things, you can tell, just will not fly,
this great and ponderous machine struggling
to get off the ground, her enigmatic smile:
I know, right? What were you thinking? ☆

Saigon Easter

It was the worst case scenario,
hundreds of children jacked-up
on Mountain Dew and biggie pops,
a football field sprinkled
with brightly colored eggs
filled with jelly beans
and miniature Tootsie Rolls,
the distant thud of a helicopter
coming in low over the surrounding hills
with the promise of ten thousand
more pink and yellow eggs loaded
like bullets with miniature Snickers bars,
Life Savers and Jolly Ranchers,
the thrill electric, the shock moving
through all those children
in their Easter bonnets and braids,
the small and the smaller breaking
through the barricades in a rush
as the lift ratio of that helicopter took hold,
the downdraft like some invisible fist
machine-gunning colored eggs in flashing
pink and orange tracers beneath the heavy
metal thump of chopper blades.
Most recipes for disaster look good on paper
but lose something in translation,
the children running for their lives,
the parents threatening to sue
if they could only decide who to blame
for so many good things having gone
so terribly wrong. ☆

Finding Bigfoot

I

It should come as no surprise
that technology has surpassed
our quest for the truth
about certain mythologies.

Bigfoot roaming the backwoods
is no match for the green hue
of night-vision goggles, thermal imaging
from remote control drones launched
by hand and flown at night.

What chance do the old monsters
have against side-image sonar
and deep structure graphics
in an array of bright colors
pixelated to clearly delineate
the rocks and stones themselves
at various, though precise, depths?

And yet, each show ends in resignation,
a sound bite screaming in the distance
from some animal never seen
though perfectly recorded,
the graphic voice-over measured
to the last decibel, a cry
that all but guarantees proof.

II

Video camera, check.
Tape recorder, check.
Stick for banging against trees, check.

We roll at dusk on four-wheelers
that slip through the dark night
like shadows through the shade,
headlights flashing the rutted trail
of some old logging road where a local
claimed he got the holy Beelzebub
scared out of him not a month earlier.

 "First I said it and then I did it,"
he said. "He come out of them trees
and crossed the road right in front of me."

"Them trees?" the host responds pointing.

"And then he went into them other trees.
I think he was following that old road."

"We're close on this one, boys,"
the host remarks. "I can feel it."

III
The art of squatch calling is just that.
The secret is in the duration of the call.
It only takes one, long whoop, but whoop
too long and you're wasting your time.
Whoop too often and you might as well go home.
A squatch can tell the difference every time.

I've been calling squatch professionally
for ten years. You learn a few tricks.
There's a certain cadence required
if you expect to fool a squatch.
Trust me, squatch are not easily fooled.

I'll knock on this tree a few times.
Did you catch that rhythm? It's not easy.
Now, we wait—There? Did you hear that?
There's a squatch around here, alright.

IV
Knocking takes patience and a lot of practice
if you want results. Sometimes
when I'm sitting around the house,
I'll work on my rhythm and technique.
It's in the wrists, you know, *thump*, *thump*—
wait a second—*thump*. Sometime*s* *thump*—
wait a second—*thump thump*. Sometimes *thump*—
wait a second—*thump*—wait a second—*thump*.

If you don't get a response, try waiting
two seconds between thumps, or two seconds
between the first thump and the second thump
and only one second between the second thump
and the third thump.

You do the math. It can get pretty complicated,
but if you spend enough time in the woods at night,
you'll get the hang of it. Work on your technique.
A lot of people think it's just *thumpthumpthump*,
but that's not it. That's not it at all.
You won't see many squatch with a rhythm like that.

V
The unknown is never as easy
as a trail of plaster cast footprints

leading toward the known, traipsing
about the woods at night, knocking
sticks together, pouring plaster of Paris.

Being a professional in this business
has more to do with effort than skill,
a cloud of coyotes howling in the distance.

"Did you hear that?" the host says.
"That first coyote didn't sound like a coyote."

Success in the squatch game comes
with no guarantees, even with a camera
that can spot a warm body at night
from outer space, the woods filled
with opossum and raccoon, two young deer.

"I can't believe this," the host says.
He lowers the camera on loan from NASA.
"It's like they knew we were coming."

"I'm not surprised," his sidekick responds
off camera. "Everyone knows Squatch
is the smartest creature in these woods." ☆

Copperhead

In some cultures, they call moving
to a new home—killing the snakes.

If you've ever lived with snakes,
you don't have to ask.

It's better to go looking
than wait until you find one
at your feet.

Either way, blood is blood,
a strange comfort, lifting
the dead weight of the thing
with a hoe and tossing it
over the fence. ☆

The Catherine Wheel

I

Walter finds himself drifting
through a strange house
toward the smell of coffee.

All his days are the same day.
A woman takes him by the arm
and eases him into his chair.

"You were supposed to call," she says,
"when you were ready to get up."

"I called and I called."

"You fall and break your hip again
and you're on your own, mister."

"What day is this?"

"Tuesday," she says. "Are you ready
for your paper?"

II

The woman sets the paper before him
and goes about her business.
She butters a piece of toast,
freshens her coffee and sits
across from him at the table
to watch him read.

He is a ghost of the man
she married, hardly able
to remember she makes his coffee
for him every morning of the week.

At some point, she will have to pull
a pair of socks on his feet,
help him into his pants and remind
him again that his name is Walter
and that she is his wife.

"Walter," he says as if he has heard
the name before. "Walter who?"

"Walter what-does-it-matter?" she smiles.
"I'll just have to remind you again later."

III

Walter opens the paper and scans the headlines.
More than anything, he is surprised
to find the world unchanged.
A two-story building is on fire.
There are young people in the street.

"At my age," he says, turning to the obituaries,
"no news is good news—" and then he sees her.

She is staring at him
from the paper in his lap.
Her hair has softened and lost
its color, but he recognizes her.

She is smiling that same smile
he had thought of fondly
so many times over the years,
the look in her eye still offering
what might have been.

IV

As old men sometimes do,
Walter is caught off-guard
by some sudden, unknown sadness,
and he realizes there are tears in his eyes.
He is crying but he can't remember why.

"Are you crying?" the woman pouring coffee asks.

"Yes," Walter says. "I don't know why."

"Is it something in the paper?"
She reads over his shoulder,
"Mary Catherine Dotson died last night
after a long struggle with cancer."
She scans down the page. "Surrounded
by her immediate family."

"Mary Catherine," Walter says to himself.

"I've heard the name," the woman says,
"but I don't recognize the face."

"A long struggle with cancer," Walter says.

He isn't sure he knows what that means.
"Does that make you sad?" the woman asks.

"Yes," Walter says.

"It makes me sad, too," she says.

V
Walter and Mary had found each other
too late, though it shouldn't have mattered.
Mary wanted to leave anyway, move away
and start over. "Start from scratch,"
she used to say with a laugh.

But Walter knew scratch.
Walter had been raised on scratch.
He didn't want to start over.
He wanted to get up and go to his job
and come home and watch television.
He wanted a life safe in a way
starting from scratch was not.

Had they not taken enough chances?
Having an affair was risky business,
and getting caught would have left him
with less than scratch—unemployed,
ostracized from his church
and his friends at Rotary.

Those were dangerous days, exciting
for being so completely filled with lust.
They were the happiest days of his life.

VI

Mary Catherine was a pure smoke factory
with her arms around his neck
and a dozen ideas for what they should do
on an afternoon all to themselves.
They could sneak off for a picnic
or drive to the city and watch a movie,
pretend in some nice restaurant
they were a couple like all the other couples.

And later, in the hotel, or in the backseat
of his car on the side of the road:
"Let's pretend I'm a good girl," she says
smiling that smile he could never resist.
"A good girl wouldn't sit in the backseat
of a car with a boy. Good girls don't do that."

"No, they do not," Walter says.

VII

"What is it, Walter? Are you crying?"

"Yes," Walter says, though he doesn't know why.
Something in the paper made him sad.

"Was it the woman," his wife asks,
"the woman who died of cancer?"

"Yes," Walter says. He is drifting again,
clerking at his father-in-law's bank.
There is a manager's position waiting for him

with an office upstairs that offers the view
of a future that doesn't involve suffering
the consequences of one bad decision.
The constant forgiveness would be a life sentence.

VIII
A blue-haired lady with fingers
like sausages bends over her organ.
With the touch of a button, the salsa
beat that had kept the room moving
dies, a high-hat cymbal sizzling
as the song resolves, replaced
by a blues number in a minor key.

It wasn't the Knights Inn
but it wasn't the Hilton,
the cheap decor backlit in amber
as Walter leans across the table
and says what he came to say.

"I don't care about any of that,"
she says. "I only care about us.
Is this what you really want?"

"Yes," Walter says. "This is what I want."

"But you're unhappy. Do you really want
to be miserable for the rest of your life?"

The blue-haired lady struck a chord.
She sang, "Now you say you're lonely."
Her sullen voice filled the lounge.

IX

"I know it's sad," the woman
who claims she is his wife says,
"but life is sad. No one lives
without regret." She takes the paper
as if it were an afterthought
and sets it off to the side.

"I don't know how else to get through to you,"
she says. "If you don't start getting better,
I'll have to put you in one of those homes.
Is that what you want?"

"No," Walter says.

"You don't even have your pants on.
You should at least put some pants on."

X

Walter sits on the edge of the bed.
He is holding something in his hands
but he isn't sure what, a brown
length of cloth, a leather belt.

"Don't just sit there," the woman says,
"they won't put themselves on."

"Pants," Walter says to himself.
His feet sit flat on the floor.
He cannot figure this whole thing out.
There is a wrinkled sock on his right foot.

The toes on his left foot look
like someone else's toes. His left foot
looks like someone else's left foot.
Walter wonders how he came to have a sock
on one foot and bare toes on the other.
Life is full of dark mysteries, he thinks.

XI
All of Walter's nights are the same night,
lying in bed, half-continent and calling
for the woman who takes him to the bathroom.
She tells him when to put his pants on
and when to take his pants off.

"It's time for bed, dear," she says.
"You have to take your pants off."

Was there something sad about today?
Walter thinks. It seems there was something
but he couldn't remember what.
No news is good news, he thinks, closing his eyes.
Maybe tomorrow he will remember
what it was that he forgot.

XII
New pain is nothing compared to old pain,
she thinks as the coffee brews.
She had been young, once, too.
She steps outside and bends with a groan
for the morning paper.

There is a chill in the air
and some half-forgotten song repeating
itself in the back of her mind.
"Now you say you're lonely," she sings softly.

She has accepted grief as his last emotion.
Loss, love and regret, there would come a day
when even these were beyond her reach.
Would it matter, for one last glimpse,
if she replaced the obituary page
with the obituaries from the day before?
Would it really matter to anyone
if Mary Catherine died again of cancer? ☆

III

Dialogue from the Land of Shovels

I have come from the land of shovels
where absence is a hole in the ground,
a conspiracy based on silence
and the dirt beneath your fingernails.

> *Do not believe what you have heard.*
> *No line divides these deadly sins*
> *from what were once cardinal virtues.*
> *There is no right or wrong here.*

I have come from the land of shovels
where the appearance of the thing
is the thing itself, the expression
on any given face a tell.

> *Do not believe what you have seen.*
> *These are not lines but scars,*
> *the memory of what you most desired*
> *in an empty field of reeds.*

I have come from the land of shovels
to confess these words are only words.
There is no moral path to follow here,
no score to settle between us.

> *Do not be distracted by what you have read.*
> *Truth comes and goes as it pleases.*
> *You must take each step with care*
> *and cut corners to make things right.* ☆

Anywhere Alaska

I

It may be because he had never been,
but from the longing in his voice,
I got the impression absence
wasn't the problem but being
too familiar, knowing
the place too well, seeing
that barren landscape
when he closed his eyes
as if it were before him,
as if he could touch it
had he only reached out his hand
toward the flat white tundra
stretching into the distance,
the horizon guarded
by mountains and snow.

II

It must have been something
the first time, to see
where the earth meets the sky.
"Your father would go anywhere
in Alaska," Mom said
after he got sick,
and I knew it was true.
There must have been something
about the feel of the cold
that came to his mind
at the end, made him close
his eyes at just the mention
of the word.

III

It was the place he wanted most
to go, only this time we would all
go together, my seventy-three-year-old mother
and me and my wife, who was back home
in Kentucky, our four grown boys
and their girlfriends, my older brother
and his second wife, who never travels,
my younger sister and her husband,
the Methodist preacher, who travel
but only stay in the best hotels
and complain the whole time
about room service.

All of us together
in one big caravan
heading north from Oklahoma
toward the Arctic Circle, the outer
limits of the civilized world,
my sister and her husband
in their new minivan
with their two sheltered kids,
my brother with a bottle of vodka
under the seat and his second wife
driving.

IV

"Anyone who wants to go,"
my father said, "can go—
uncles and aunts, cousins, friends.
You can camp if you want,
or stay in a hotel."

"That would be something," I said,
knowing what I knew about the progression
of the disease and the complications
growing, already, more apparent,
the circumstance that made me leave
my wife and job in Kentucky
for Central Standard Time.

"You have to see it
to believe it," my father said.
"Nothing but snow and blue sky
as far as the eye can see."

"That would be something," I said,
knowing what I knew
about the likelihood
of us all coming together
for a trip to anywhere
Alaska, caravanning our way
across the great plains
into Canada, driving and
driving and driving
to get somewhere that might
bring us all together
for one last look
at the mountains
in the distance.

V

The night my father died,
an ice storm hit Tulsa.
The Storm of the Century,
they said on the news.
It buried everything
beneath four inches of ice,
the houses and the trees,
the roads and telephone poles,
ditches and manicured lawns.

The whole world turned white.
The airport shut down
for days, the churches
and cemeteries even longer.
No one could get in
and no one could get out,
the ground frozen solid
beneath a white sheet of ice
that stretched as far
as the eye could see
into the blue and empty sky. ☆

Moondogs

I

I have dreamed this dream before,
though it is never the same dream.
The bark of the moondogs echo
through the memory song of desire,
the wet slick pavement in the parking lot
of the cancer ward dripping in moonlight.
There is the sound that water makes
and there is the sound that water makes,
the gutter wash of another dark night
caught in the bare branch of a tree.

II

While my father was dying of cancer,
I slept on a fold-out cot
and dreamed Death a huckster
in a white jumpsuit and cape,
his lapels inlaid with faux diamonds
and imitation pearls.

I didn't want the real thing.
I wanted cubic zirconia,
a scarf of glass rubies.
I wanted something I could hold up
and say, *Here is the monster we face,*
languishing behind the ultimate disguise
of himself in full regalia. His body convulsed
to the rattle and roll of a pelvic hot
swivel in the hips, his gilded belt buckle
and snakeskin shoes seductive, slip-sliding
to the tune of some bargained for melody

of love and loss, the having and the holding,
followed always by dread.

III
Death is a fancy dancer. He moves
like a slow motion bolt of lightning,
like water running downhill, raising
his outstretched hand and taking hold
of what potential exists for the desired
boogie effect, his cape fluttering as he lifts
himself twisting in a mambo flair and groove.
His feet shuffle to a rhythm watusi,
hips wheeling in great swirls of attraction,
whirling in a mesmerized jitterbug
of motion. The Mashed Potato, the Funky Monkey,
the Alligator Crawl, he knows them all.
He slips from one smooth step to the next
with a tango kick and dip as the ladies scream.
He raises one eyebrow and they faint
in full swoon for having come, at last,
and been taken in by that southern crooning
voice. There is faith abounding in his honey
sweet song, softly ballad and moving
full-throated and silver-tongued devilwards.
He is the fruit of our own choosing,
having been taught to believe in the garbled
word at the back of the throat, in the fiction
that is our lives, though the light from the moon
is only the light from the moon, small
and ghostwhite in the blueblack sky.

IV

The last thing my father said before he died
was I think I'm going to beat this thing.
One door closes and another door opens.
I knew, then, there was such a thing
as deception in this world. I pulled
at the sheets to help him turn in bed
and tried not to imagine what the doctor meant
when he held out his hands and said,
"This is where we are,
and this is where we are going,"
the silence between each hand
like the bark of a dog.

I had no choice but look away
from this stranger in his white suit,
with his perfect hair and smile.
I had no choice but accept the distance
between each hand as an unmeasured thing.

V

If there is a key to the secret of the mystery,
it is showmanship: the concerned touch,
the cautious smile. Never mind there is blood
on your hands, the stars too numerous to count
as the breath grows more strenuous and labored,
pushing its way through a gloomy film of words.
Moonlight washes across the night sky.
The walls of the hospital room turn
their blue shoulders from the beat of the machines,
the improbability of success seductive

as it creeps slowly back from the edge of hope,
one hand rising to a lengthening note
carried high above the splendor
as he goes low with a swooping gesture
and drops to one knee, his long fingers
maneuvering his cape with a flourish,
as if it were waving in a wind
only my father could feel,
the darkness growing more pervasive.

If there is a key to the secret of the mystery,
it is knowing there is no resisting
this songster evil as we listen, enthralled
as the same misfortune recurs with remarkable ease,
just the hint of a smile on his twisted lip
as he raises one hand in patterns potentially limitless
but always the same, the final act repeating itself
in varying degrees of separation but always
with the same flair, his perfect teeth
glittering in the artificial light,
his shuffle dance moving steadily toward the inevitable
low-stooped bow, the before and the after
like a vanishing ghost, all the grand gestures
connecting nothing to nothing but illusion,
smoke and mirrors caught in the circular yes
and yes of the somewhere else, the definite maybe,
the connotative perhaps, though the blood
looks real and the irony seems intentional,
the perpetrator of the crime caught in some wild
previosity, ignoring all accusations.

VI

There is a new monster in town,
one born for every age, the self-imagined self
looking back with benevolence and compassion
beneath the ghostbody of another full moon,
the long, slow years of wear grasped
in that last, unforgiven moment.

There is an evil in this world
that comes with a swirl in his cape,
his words sliding by like a compromise
never reached. And so we wait,
bleary-eyed and tired to the bone,
sitting in this hospital room
as the moondogs gather. ☆

My Father on the Fire Tower

He's a young man in the photograph,
    leaning into the swagger of youth
    with his shirt tucked into his jeans
    and his sleeves cuffed. The casual flip
    in his hair seems almost effortless,
    though there's no escaping that steel geography,
    the sky behind triangular with crossbars and beams
    as he leans against the rail and smiles.

I was a boy when the picture was taken,
    afraid to follow him any higher
    for the uncertain sway of those metal steps.
    Despite his assurance that everything would be fine,
    I held to the rail and didn't look down,
    the hills stretching into the distance
    like the upturned palm of his hand
    across the wide angle of our lives.

Imagine my surprise when I look down
    and realize it wasn't my father who got old.
    These babies that cling to my knees
    are not my children but my grandchildren,
    asking will I lift them up in the air.
    And I do because that's what they need.
    I know this ground as sure as I know
    the voice I hear calling for me to follow
    and not be afraid, each measured step
    a homecoming. ☆

ACKNOWLEDGEMENTS

My grateful acknowledgment is extended to the following people and organizations for their support: The Kentucky Arts Council, The Ohio Arts Council, The National Endowment for the Arts, Virginia Underwood, poet Audrey Naffziger for her invaluable editorial support, the visual artists Mark Hackworth and Steve Ward for their collaboration on *The Pfeilstorch Incident and Other Conspiracies*, an art exhibit which lead to many of the poems in this collection.

"Copperhead" appeared in *The Pikeville Review: A Journal of Contemporary Appalachian Literature* (Spring, 2015).

"My Father on the Firetower" appeared in "Crossing Country Line by Line." YARN, National Poetry Month project: Pennsylvania & Beyond (2012).

"Theories of Elegance" appeared in *The Journal of Kentucky Studies* (September 1998).

The title page photograph is that of Thomas Amos and Grace Langan, my grandparents on my mother's side. I took this photograph of them sitting on the porch of their farmhouse on the outskirts of Manford, Oklahoma, in the summer of 1963. You can see my shadow on the wall of the porch behind my grandmother's chair—just to the right of her hand, raised to shield her eyes from the bright sunlight.

James Alan Riley is an American poet. He is the recipient of a National Endowment for the Arts Fellowship, two Al Smith Individual Artist Fellowships from the Kentucky Arts Council, and an Individual Artist Fellowship from the Ohio Arts Council. He edited *Kentucky Voices: A Collection of Contemporary Kentucky Short Stories* (PC Press, 1997). His work has appeared in *The Louisville Review, Kentucky Monthly, The Journal of Kentucky Studies, Appalachian Heritage, The Connecticut Review, The Greensboro Review, West Branch,* and a number of other literary magazines over the years. Riley received his Ph.D. in Modern British and American Literature from Ohio University in Athens and a Masters in English from the University of Arkansas. He is currently the English Program Coordinator and a Professor of English at the University of Pikeville in Pikeville, Kentucky, where he has taught since 1987.